BASICS OF GO PROGRAMMING

DR DHEERAJ MEHROTRA

Contents

Preface

*Basics of **Go** Programming is a module for basics for beginners. It is expected to deliver a learning module with sample codes of programming skills using simple examples.*

Let us do the Go Programming.

Happy Learning Guys!

Dheeraj Mehrotra

CHAPTER I

Programming in Go Language

Go is a statically typed, compiled programming language designed at Google by
Robert Griesemer, Rob Pike, and Ken Thompson.
Most similarly modelled after C, Go is statically typed and explicit.

Go (also called Golang or Go language) is an open source programming language used **for general purpose**.
Go was developed by Google engineers to create dependable and efficient software.

Go beats Python by far. Go even beats Java's speed, which is widely considered to be significantly faster than Python. If it comes down to needing a program to load software quickly, Go is the way to Go

Go is **an open-source programming language** focused on simplicity, reliability, and efficiency. Go became an open-source project and was released publicly in 2012. It quickly gained a surprising level of popularity and has become one of the leading modern programming languages.

Go's syntax is small compared to other languages, and **it's easy to learn**. You can fit most of it in your head, which means you don't need to spend a lot of time looking things up. It's also very clean and easy-to-read.

4

Go language's design teaches us how to solve engineering problems with minimal and complete solutions.

To the surprise of many, Go has only 25 keywords, but it offers all features that you need to build any software system. Just imaging, 25 keywords are enough to design a full-featured programming language.

```
package main
import ("fmt")

func main() {
  fmt.Println("Hi, Welcome to Go Programming")
}
```

```
Hi, Welcome to Go Programming
```

What is Go?

Go is a cross-platform, open-source programming language

- Go can be used to create high-performance applications
- Go is a fast, statically typed, compiled language that feels like a dynamically typed, interpreted language
- Go was developed at Google by Robert Griesemer, Rob Pike, and Ken Thompson in 2007
- Go's syntax is similar to C++

What is Go Used For?

- Web development (server-side)
- Developing network-based programs
- Developing cross-platform enterprise applications
- Cloud-native development

Why Use Go?

- Go is fun and easy to learn
- Go has a fast run time and compilation time
- Go supports concurrency
- Go has a memory management
- Go works on different platforms (Windows, Mac, Linux, Raspberry Pi, etc.)

Getting Started with Go!

To start using Go, you need two things:
- A text editor, like VS Code, to write Go code
- A compiler, like GCC, to translate the Go code into a language that the computer will understand.

Installation of Go Compiler

You can find the relevant installation files at https://golang.org/dl/.

Follow the instructions related to your operating system. To check if Go was installed successfully, you can run the following command in a terminal window:

```
go version
```

This shall show the version of your **Go** installation.

Installation of IDE

An IDE (Integrated Development Environment) is used to edit AND compile the code.

Popular IDE's include Visual Studio Code (VS Code), Vim, Eclipse, and Notepad. These are all free, and they can be used to both edit and debug Go code.

Sample Program: Welcome to programming in Go!

```go
package main
import ("fmt")

func main() {
   fmt.Println("Welcome to programming in Go!")
}
```

Understanding the Sample Program

Line 1: In Go, every program is part of a package. We define this using the `package` keyword. In this example, the program belongs to the `main` package.

Line 2: `import ("fmt")` lets us import files included in the `fmt` package.

Line 3: A blank line. Go ignores white space. Having white spaces in code makes it more readable.

Line 4: `func main() {}` is a function. Any code inside its curly brackets `{}` will be executed.

Line 5: `fmt.Println()` is a function made available from the `fmt` package. It is used to output/print text. In our example, it will output "Welcome to programming in Go!"

```go
package main
import ("fmt")

func main() {
    fmt.Println("Welcome to programming in Go!")
}
```

Go Statements

`fmt.Println("Hello World!")` is a statement.

In Go, statements are separated by ending a line (hitting the Enter key) or by a semicolon ";".

Hitting the Enter key adds ";" to the end of the line implicitly (does not show up in the source code).

The left curly bracket { cannot come at the start of a line.

fmt stands for the Format package. The fmt allows to format basic strings, values, or anything and print them.
It also collects the user input from the console, writes it into a file using a writer. It also in addition allows a print customized fancy error messages. This package is all about formatting input and output within a program in GO.

Go Statements

`fmt.Println("Hello World!")` is a statement.

In Go, statements are separated by ending a line (hitting the Enter key) or by a semicolon ";".

Hitting the Enter key adds ";" to the end of the line implicitly

The left curly bracket { cannot come at the start of a line.

```go
package main
import ("fmt")

func main()
{
  fmt.Println("Hello World!")
}
```

Go Comments

Line any computer programming language, A comment is a text that is ignored upon execution and can be used to explain the code, and to make it more readable.

Comments can also be used to prevent code execution when testing an alternative code. Go supports single-line or multi-line comments.

Go Single-line Comments
Single-line comments start with two forward slashes (//).
Any text between // and the end of the line is ignored by the compiler (will not be executed).
```go
// This is a comment
```

```go
func main() {
  // This is a comment
  fmt.Println("Hello World!")
}
```

Go Multi-line Comments

Multi-line comments start with /* and ends with */.
Any text between /* and */ will be ignored by the
compiler:

```go
package main
import ("fmt")

func main() {
/* The code below will print Hello, How are you?
to the screen, and it is amazing */
  fmt.Println("Hello, How are you?")
}
```

Go Variable Types

In Go, there are different **types** of variables, for example:

* `int`- stores integers (whole numbers), such as 123 or -123
* `float32`- stores floating-point numbers, with decimals, such as 19.99 or -19.99
* `string` - stores text, such as "Hello World". String values are surrounded by double quotes
* `bool`- stores values with two states: true or false

Declaring (Creating) Variables

In Go, there are two ways to declare a variable:

1. With the `var` keyword:
Use the `var` keyword, followed by variable name and type:
Syntax
`var variablename type = value`

Note: You always have to specify either `type` or `value` (or both).

2. With the `:=` sign:
Use the `:=` sign, followed by the variable value:
Syntax
`variablename := value`

Note: It is not possible to declare a variable using `:=`, without assigning a value to it.

Variable Declaration With Initial Value

If the value of a variable is known from the start, you can declare the variable and assign a value to it on one line:

Example

```go
package main
import ("fmt")
// Program to display the value of any assigned value

func main() {
  var student1 string = "Amit Gupta" //type is string
  var student2 = "Sumit Gupta" //type is inferred
  x := 200 //type is inferred

  fmt.Println(student1)
  fmt.Println(student2)
  fmt.Println(x)
}
```

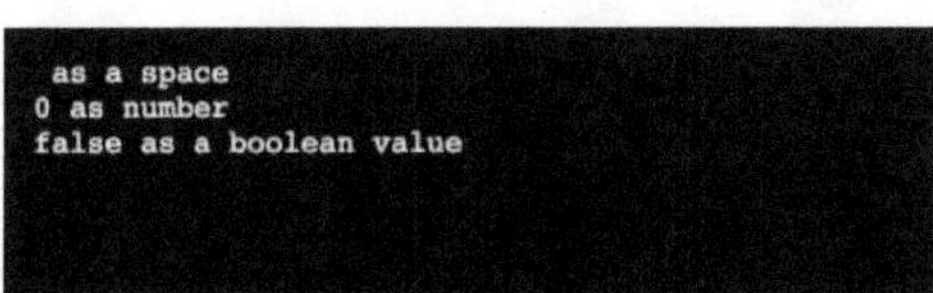

Variable Declaration Without Initial Value

In Go, all variables are initialized. So, if you declare a variable without an initial value, its value will be set to the default value of its type:

```go
package main
import ("fmt")

func main() {
  var a string
  var b int
  var c bool

  fmt.Println(a, "as a space")
  fmt.Println(b, "as number")
  fmt.Println(c, "as a boolean value")
}
```

Value Assignment After Declaration

It is possible to assign a value to a variable after it is declared. This is helpful for cases the value is not initially known.

Example

```go
package main
import ("fmt")

func main() {
  var student1 string
  student1 = "Amit Gupta"
  fmt.Println(student1)
}
```

Difference Between var and :=

There are some small differences between the var var :=:

var
:=
Can be used **inside** and **outside** of functions
Can only be used **inside** functions
Variable declaration and value assignment **can be done separately**
Variable declaration and value assignment **cannot be done separately** (must be done in the same line)

Sample Program Code:

```go
package main
import ("fmt")

var a int
var b int = 200
var c = 300

func main() {
  a = 100
  fmt.Println(a)
  fmt.Println(b)
  fmt.Println(c)
}
```

Go Multiple Variable Declaration

In Go, it is possible to declare multiple variables in the same line.

```go
package main
import ("fmt")

func main() {
  var aa, bb, cc, dd int = 100, 300, 500, 700

  fmt.Println("The value of 'aa' is",aa)
  fmt.Println("The value of 'bb' is",bb)
  fmt.Println("The value of 'cc' is",cc)
  fmt.Println("The value of 'dd' is",dd)
}
```

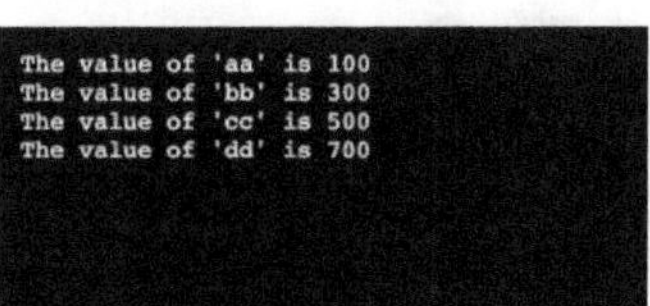

If the `type` **keyword is not specified, you can declare different types of variables in the same line:**

```go
package main
import ("fmt")

func main() {
  var a, b = 10, "Hey Guys!"
  c, d := 25, "How are you?"

  fmt.Println(a)
  fmt.Println(b)
  fmt.Println(c)
  fmt.Println(d)
}
```

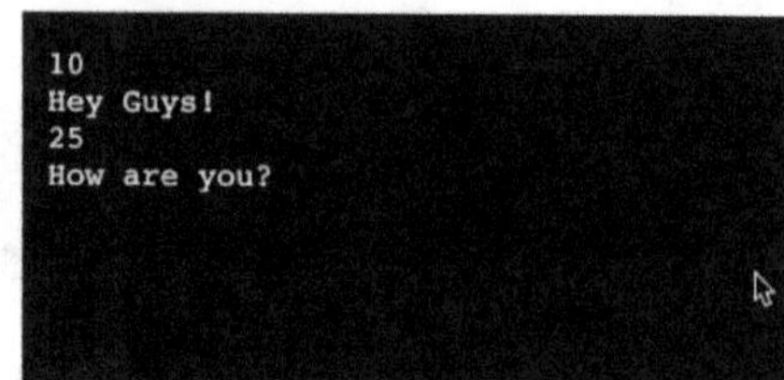

Go Variable Declaration in a Block

Multiple variable declarations can also be grouped together into a block for greater readability:

```go
package main
import ("fmt")

func main() {
  var (
    a int
    b int = 100
    c string = "Hi, How are you doing?"
  )

  fmt.Println(a, " is the value of a")
  fmt.Println(b, " is the value of b")
  fmt.Println(c, " is the value of c")
}
```

Go Variable Naming Rules

A variable can have a short name (like x and y) or a more descriptive name (age, price, carname, etc.).

Go variable naming rules:

- A variable name must start with a letter or an underscore character (_)
- A variable name cannot start with a digit
- A variable name can only contain alpha-numeric characters and underscores (a-z, A-Z, 0-9, and _)
- Variable names are case-sensitive (age, Age and AGE are three different variables)
- There is no limit on the length of the variable name
- A variable name cannot contain spaces
- The variable name cannot be any Go keywords

Multi-Word Variable Names

Variable names with more than one word can be difficult to read.

There are several techniques you can use to make them more readable:

Camel Case

Each word, except the first, starts with a capital letter:

```
myVariableName = "Abhishek"
```

Pascal Case

Each word starts with a capital letter:

```
MyVariableName = "Abhishek"
```

Snake Case

Each word is separated by an underscore character:

```
my_variable_name = "Abhishek"
```

Go Constants

If a variable should have a fixed value that cannot be changed, you can use the const keyword.

The const keyword declares the variable as "constant", which means that it is **unchangeable and read-only**.

Syntax

```
const CONSTNAME type = value
```

Declaring a Constant

Here is an example of declaring a constant in Go:

Example

```
package main
import ("fmt")
// Use of const variable
const PI = 3.14

func main() {
  fmt.Println(PI, "is the value of PI")
}
```

```
3.14 is the value of PI
```

Constant Rules
- Constant names follow the same naming rules as <u>variables</u>
- Constant names are usually written in uppercase letters (for easy identification and differentiation from variables)
- Constants can be declared both inside and outside of a function

Constant Types
There are two types of constants:

- Typed constants
- Untyped constants

Typed Constants
Typed constants are declared with a defined type:

Untyped Constants
Untyped constants are declared without a type:

```go
package main
import ("fmt")

const Amount = 1000

func main() {
  fmt.Println("Amount is",Amount)
}
```

```
Amount is 1000
```

Constants: Unchangeable and Read-only

When a constant is declared, it is not possible to change the value later:

Example

```go
package main
import ("fmt")

func main() {
  const Amount = 1000
  Amount = 2000
  fmt.Println("The value of Amount is ",Amount)
}
```

```
# _/home/hK4uvE
./prog.go:6:10: cannot assign to Amount
```

Multiple Constants Declaration

Multiple constants can be grouped together into a block for readability:

The sample code is :

```go
package main
import ("fmt")

const (
 A int = 100
 B = 3.14
 C = "Hi! Dear How are you?"
)

func main() {
 fmt.Println(A, " is the value of A")
 fmt.Println(B," is the value of B" )
 fmt.Println(C, " is the value of C")
}
```

```
100  is the value of A
3.14  is the value of B
Hi! Dear How are you?  is the value of C
```

Go Output Functions

Go has three functions to output text:

* Print()
* Println()
* Printf()

The Print() Function

The Print() function prints its arguments with their default format, as per the example:

```go
package main
import ("fmt")

func main() {
 var i,j string = "Hello, How are you ","My Dear Friend"

 fmt.Print(i)// Prints i
 fmt.Print(j)// Prints j
}
```

```
Hello, How are you My Dear Friend
```

```go
package main
import ("fmt")

func main() {
 var i,j string = "Hello, How are you ","My Dear Friend"

 fmt.Print(i)// Prints i
 fmt.Print("\n")// Prints a new line
 fmt.Print("\n") // Prints a new line
 fmt.Print(j)// Prints j
}
```

```
Hello, How are you

My Dear Friend
```

The Println() Function

The `Println()` function is similar to `Print()` with the difference that a whitespace is added between the arguments, and a newline is added at the end:

```go
package main
import ("fmt")

func main() {
  var i,j string = "Hello, How are you ","My Dear Friend"

  fmt.Println(i)// Prints i
          fmt.Println()// Prints an extra line
  fmt.Println(j)// Prints j
}
```

```
Hello, How are you

My Dear Friend
```

General Formatting Verbs

The following verbs can be used with all data types:

Verb/ Description

%v   Prints the value in the default format

%#v Prints the value in Go-syntax format

%T   Prints the type of the value

%%   Prints the % sign

```go
package main
import ("fmt")

func main() {
  var i = 98.4
  var txt = "Hi, All. Welcome to the world of programming!"

  fmt.Printf("%v\n", i)
  fmt.Printf("%#v\n", i)
  fmt.Printf("%v%%\n", i)
  fmt.Printf("%T\n", i)

  fmt.Printf("%v\n", txt)
  fmt.Printf("%#v\n", txt)
  fmt.Printf("%T\n", txt)
}
```

```
98.4
98.4
98.4%
float64
Hi, All. Welcome to the world of programming!
"Hi, All. Welcome to the world of programming!"
string
```

Integer Formatting Verbs

The following verbs can be used with the integer data type:

Verb	Description
%b	Base 2
%d	Base 10
%+d	Base 10 and always show sign
%o	Base 8
%O.	Base 8, with leading 0o
%x.	Base 16, lowercase
%X.	Base 16, uppercase
%#x.	Base 16, with leading 0x
%4d	Pad with spaces (width 4, right-justified)
%-4d	Pad with spaces (width 4, left-justified)
%04d.	Pad with zeroes (width 4

```go
package main
import ("fmt")

func main() {
 var i = 2510

 fmt.Printf("%b\n", i)// Base 2
 fmt.Printf("%d\n", i) // Base 10
 fmt.Printf("%+d\n", i) // Base 10 and sign
 fmt.Printf("%O\n", i) // Base 8
 fmt.Printf("%x\n", i) // Base 16, lowercase
 fmt.Printf("%o\n", i) // Base 8, with leading os.
 fmt.Printf("%X\n", i) // Base 16, uppercase
 fmt.Printf("%#x\n", i) // Base 16, with leading ox
 fmt.Printf("%4d\n", i) // Pad with spaces (width 4, right-justified)
 fmt.Printf("%-4d\n", i) // Pad with spaces (width 4, left-justified)
 fmt.Printf("%04d\n", i) // Pad with zeroes (width 4)

}
```

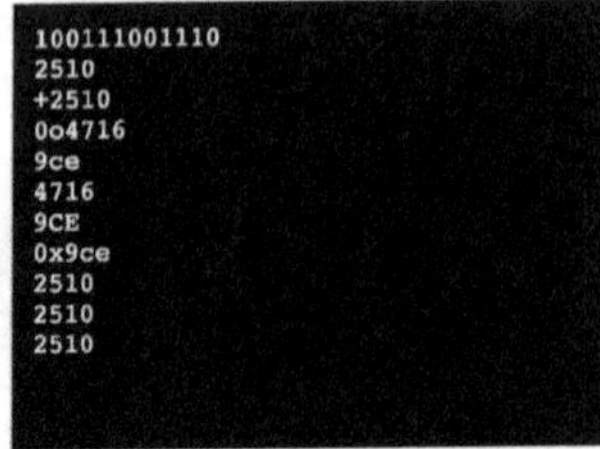

String Formatting Verbs

The following verbs can be used with the string data type:

Verb/ Description

%s   Prints the value as plain string

%q   Prints the value as a double-quoted string

%8s Prints the value as plain string (width 8, right justified)

%-8s Prints the value as plain string (width 8, left justified)

%x   Prints the value as hex dump of byte values

% x   Prints the value as hex dump with spaces

```go
package main
import ("fmt")

func main() {
 var txt = "Programming in GO"

 fmt.Printf("%s\n", txt) // Prints the value as plain string
 fmt.Printf("%q\n", txt) // Prints the value as a double-quoted string
 fmt.Printf("%8s\n", txt) // Prints the value as plain string (width 8, right justified)
 fmt.Printf("%-8s\n", txt) // Prints the value as plain string (width 8, left justified)
 fmt.Printf("%x\n", txt)  // Prints the value as hex dump of byte values
 fmt.Printf("% x\n", txt)  // Prints the value as hex dump with spaces
}
```

```
Programming in GO
"Programming in GO"
Programming in GO
Programming in GO
50726f6772616d6d696e6720696e20474f
50 72 6f 67 72 61 6d 6d 69 6e 67 20 69 6e 20 47 4f
```

Boolean Formatting Verbs

The following verb can be used with the boolean data type:

Verb/ Description
%t   Value of the boolean operator in
         true or false format
         (same as using %v)

```go
package main
import ("fmt")
// Boolean showcase
func main() {
 var a = false
 var b = true

 fmt.Printf("%t\n", a)
 fmt.Printf("%t\n", b)
}
```

Boolean Formatting Verbs

The following verb can be used with the boolean data type:

Verb/ Description

%t   Value of the boolean operator in
          true or false format
          (same as using %v)

```go
package main
import ("fmt")
// Boolean showcase
func main() {
 var a = false
 var b = true

 fmt.Printf("%t\n", a)
 fmt.Printf("%t\n", b)
}
```

Float Formatting Verbs

The following verbs can be used with the float data type:

Verb/ Description

%e.   Scientific notation with 'e' as an exponent
%f.   Decimal point, no exponent
%.2f. Default width, precision 2
%6.2f.Width 6, precision 2
%g   Exponent as needed, only necessary digits

```go
package main
import ("fmt")

func main() {
  var i = 98.4
  var txt = "Hey Boys, How are you all?"

  fmt.Printf("%v\n", i)  // Prints the value in the default format
  fmt.Printf("%#v\n", i) // Prints the value in Go-syntax format
  fmt.Printf("%v%%\n", i) // Prints the type of the value
  fmt.Printf("%T\n", i)

  fmt.Printf("%v\n", txt) // Prints the value in the default format
  fmt.Printf("%#v\n", txt) // Prints the value in Go-syntax format
  fmt.Printf("%T\n", txt) // Prints the type of the value
}
```

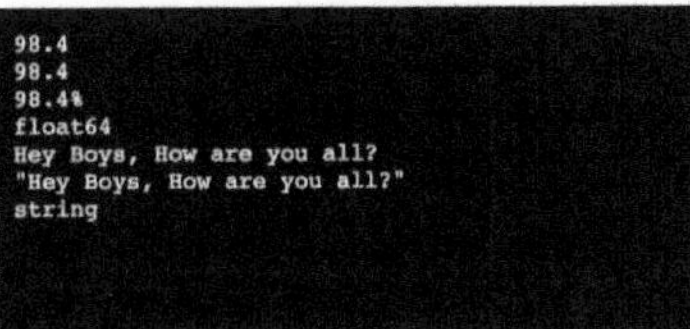

Go Data Types

Data type is an important concept in programming. Data type specifies the size and type of variable values.

Go is statically typed, meaning that once a variable type is defined, it can only store data of that type.

Go has three basic data types:
- **bool**: represents a boolean value and is either true or false
- **Numeric**: represents integer types, floating point values, and complex types
- **string**: represents a string value

```
package main
import ("fmt")

func main() {
  var a bool = true     // Boolean Value
  var b int = 500       // Integer Value
  var c float32 = 3.14  // Floating point number
  var d string = "Hi! How are you?" // String Value

  fmt.Println("Boolean: ", a)
  fmt.Println("Integer: ", b)
  fmt.Println("Float:   ", c)
  fmt.Println("String:  ", d)
}
```

```
Boolean:   true
Integer:   500
Float:     3.14
String:    Hi! How are you?
```

Boolean Data Type

A boolean data type is declared with the `bool` keyword and can only take the values `true` or `false`.

The default value of a boolean data type is `false`.

```go
package main
import ("fmt")

func main() {
    var boy1 bool = true // showcase of typed declaration with initial value
    var boy2 = true // showcase of untyped declaration with initial value
    var boy3 =false // showcase of untyped declaration without initial value
    boy4 := true // Showcase of untyped declaration with initial value

    fmt.Println(boy1) // Returns true accordingly.
    fmt.Println(boy2) // Returns true accordingly.
    fmt.Println(boy3) // Returns false accordingly.
    fmt.Println(boy4) // Returns true accordingly.
```

Go Integer Data Types

Integer data types are used to store a whole number without decimals, like 35, -50, or 1345000.

The integer data type has two categories:

- **Signed integers** - can store both positive and negative values
- **Unsigned integers** - can only store non-negative values

```go
package main
import ("fmt")

func main() {
  var x int = 12345
  var y int = -2234
  fmt.Printf("Type: %T, value: %v\n", x, x)
  fmt.Printf("Type: %T, value: %v", y, y)
}
```

```
Type: int, value: 12345
Type: int, value: -2234
```

Signed integers, declared with one of the `int` keywords, can store both positive and negative values:

```go
package main
import ("fmt")

func main() {
  var x int = 100
  var y int = -200
  fmt.Printf("Type value of : %T, value: %v", x, x)
  fmt.Println()
  fmt.Println("New Line")
  fmt.Printf("Type value of : %T, value: %v", y, y)
}
```

```
Type value of : int, value: 100
New Line
Type value of : int, value: -200
```

Go has five keywords/types of signed integers:

int	Depends on platform: 32 bits in 32 bit systems and 64 bit in 64 bit systems	-2147483648 to 2147483647 in 32 bit systems and -9223372036854775808 to 9223372036854775807 in 64 bit systems
int8	8 bits/1 byte	-128 to 127
int16	16 bits/2 byte	-32768 to 32767
int32	32 bits/4 byte	-2147483648 to 2147483647
int64	64 bits/8 byte	-9223372036854775808 to 9223372036854775807

Unsigned integers, declared with one of the uint keywords, can only store non-negative values:

```
package main
import ("fmt")

func main() {
  var x uint = 500
  var y uint = 4500
  fmt.Printf("Type Value is: %T, value: %v", x, x)
    fmt.Println()
fmt.Printf("Type Value is: %T, value: %v", y, y)
}
```

```
Type Value is: uint, value: 500
Type Value is: uint, value: 4500
```

```go
package main
import ("fmt")

func main() {
  var x uint = 100
  var y uint = 200
  fmt.Printf("Type Value is: %T, value: %v", x, x)
   fmt.Println()

  fmt.Printf("Type Value is: %T, value: %v", y, y)
}
```

```
Type Value is: uint, value: 100
Type Value is: uint, value: 200
```

Go has five keywords/types of unsigned integers:

Type	Size	Range
uint	Depends on platform: 32 bits in 32 bit systems and 64 bit in 64 bit systems	0 to 4294967295 in 32 bit systems and 0 to 18446744073709551615 in 64 bit systems
uint8	8 bits/1 byte	0 to 255
uint16	16 bits/2 byte	0 to 65535
uint32	32 bits/4 byte	0 to 4294967295
uint64	64 bits/8 byte	0 to 18446744073709551615

Go Float Data Types

The float data types are used to store positive and negative numbers with a decimal point, like 35.3, -2.34, or 3597.34987.

The float data type has two keywords:

Type	Size	Range
float32	32 bits	-3.4e+38 to 3.4e+38.
float64	64 bits	-1.7e+308 to +1.7e+308.

```
Type: is float32, value: 98.78
Type: is float32, value: 1.4e+38
```

```
package main
import ("fmt")
func main() {
  var x float32 = 98.78
  var y float32 = 1.4e+38
  fmt.Printf("Type: is %T, value: %v\n", x, x)
  fmt.Printf("Type: is %T, value: %v", y, y)
}
```

String Data Type

The `string` data type is used to store a sequence of characters (text). String values must be surrounded by double quotes:

```go
package main
import ("fmt")

func main() {
  var txt1 string = "Hello! Brother"
  var txt2 string
  txt3 := "How are you?"
  fmt.Printf("Type: %T, value: is as:: %v\n", txt1, txt1)
  fmt.Printf("Type: %T, value: is as:: %v\n", txt2, txt2)
  fmt.Printf("Type: %T, value: is as:: %v\n", txt3, txt3)
}
```

```
Type: string, value: is as:: Hello! Brother
Type: string, value: is as::
Type: string, value: is as:: How are you?
```

Go Arrays

Arrays are used to store multiple values of the same type in a single variable, unlike the variables.

In Go, there are two ways to declare an array:

1. With the `var` keyword:

Syntax

```go
var array_name = [length]datatype{values} // here length is defined
```

or

```go
var array_name = [...]datatype{values} // here length is inferred
```

2. With the `:=` sign:

Syntax

```go
array_name := [length]datatype{values} // here length is defined
```

or

```go
array_name := [...]datatype{values} // here length is inferred
```

Examples:

```
package main
import ("fmt")

func main() {
 var arr1 = [2]int{11,22}
 arr2 := [6]int{44,55,66,77,88,99}

 fmt.Println(arr1)
 fmt.Println(arr2)
}
```

```
[11 22]
[44 55 66 77 88 99]
```

```
package main
import ("fmt")
func main() {
  var arr1 = [...]int{1,2}
  arr2 := [...]int{44,55,66,77}
// PRINTING ARRAYS
  fmt.Println("THE ARRAY ONE IS",arr1)
  fmt.Println("THE ARRAY TWO IS",arr2)
}
```

```
THE ARRAY ONE IS [1 2]
THE ARRAY TWO IS [44 55 66 77]
```

STRING ARRAYS

```go
package main
import ("fmt")
// String Array

func main() {
 var employees = [4]string{"AMIT", "SUMIT", "SHASHANK", "BABLU"}
 // Printing the Array
 fmt.Print("Hey Guys", employees, "are the members of the array employees")
}
```

```
Hey Guys[AMIT SUMIT SHASHANK BABLU]are the members of the array employees
```

We can access a specific array element by referring to the index number.

In Go, array indexes start at 0. That means that [0] is the first element, [1] is the second element, accordingly.

```go
package main
import ("fmt")

func main() {

// array is defined with 4 elements with 100 being stored at zero index.
  roll := [4]int{100,220,330,440}

  fmt.Println("The element of first cell is", roll[0])
  // 0 is the first element
  fmt.Println("The element of fourth cell is",roll[3])
  // index 3 is the the fourth element
}
```

```
The element of first cell is 100
The element of fourth cell is 440
```

We can also change the value of a specific array element by referring to the index number. If an array or one of its elements has not been initialized in the code, it is assigned the default value of its type. By default: int is 0, and the default value for string is "".

Example:

```
package main
import ("fmt")
func main() {
  marks := [3]int{20,320,3220}
  marks[2] = 500 // changing cell value as 500
  fmt.Println("The value of the new array is",marks)
}
```

```
The value of the new array is [20 320 500]
```

Sample Program:
```
package main
import ("fmt")

func main() {
  arr1 := [5]int{} //not initialized
  arr2 := [5]int{11,22} //partially initialized
  arr3 := [5]int{11,12,13,14,15} //fully initialized

  fmt.Println("Not Initialized Case", arr1)
  fmt.Println("Partially Initialized Case", arr2)
  fmt.Println("Fully Initialized Case",arr3)
}
```

```
Not Initialized Case [0 0 0 0 0]
Partially Initialized Case [11 22 0 0 0]
Fully Initialized Case [11 12 13 14 15]
```

Length of an Array

The `len()` function is used to find the length of an array:

```go
package main
import ("fmt")
func main() {
  arr1 := [4]string{"Bablu", "Tannu", "James", "Sumit"}
  arr2 := [...]int{91,22,33,44,35,36}
 fmt.Println("The length of the array is",len(arr1))
  fmt.Println("The Length of the array is",len(arr2))
 }
```

```
The length of the array is 4
The Length of the array is 6
```

Go Slices

Slices are similar to arrays, but are more powerful and flexible.

Like arrays, slices are also used to store multiple values of the same type in a single variable.

However, unlike arrays, the length of a slice can grow and shrink as you see fit.

In Go, there are several ways to create a slice:

- Using the []*datatype*{*values*} format
- Create a slice from an array
- Using the make() function

In Go, there are two functions that can be used to return the length and capacity of a slice:

- `len()` function - returns the length of the slice (the number of elements in the slice)
- `cap()` function - returns the capacity of the slice (the number of elements the slice can grow or shrink to)

```go
package main
import ("fmt")

func main() {
 goslice := []int{}
 fmt.Println(len(goslice))
 fmt.Println(cap(goslice))
 fmt.Println(goslice)

 goslice2 := []string{"Go", "Is", "A", "Programming", "Language"}
 fmt.Println("The Length is",len(goslice2))
 fmt.Println("The cap value is",cap(goslice2))
 fmt.Println(goslice2)
}
```

```
0
0
[ ]
The Length is 5
The cap value is 5
[Go Is A Programming Language]
```

We can create a slice by slicing an array:

Syntax

```go
var myarray = [length]datatype{values} // An array
myslice := myarray[start:end] // A slice made from the array
```

Example:

```go
package main
import ("fmt")

func main() {
 arr1 := [6]int{50, 141, 142, 133, 134,415}
 meslice := arr1[2:4]

 fmt.Printf("The array meslice is = %v\n", meslice)
 fmt.Printf("The length is = %d\n", len(meslice))
 fmt.Printf("The capacity is = %d\n", cap(meslice))
}
```

```
The array meslice is = [142 133]
The length is = 2
The capacity is = 4
```

The make() function can also be used to create a slice.

```go
package main
import ("fmt")

func main() {
// Learning to create slices using the make() function
  meslice1 := make([]int, 4, 5) // make function
  fmt.Printf("meslice1 = %v\n", meslice1)
  fmt.Printf("length = %d\n", len(meslice1))
  fmt.Printf("capacity = %d\n", cap(meslice1))

  meslice2 := make([]int, 6)  // make function
  fmt.Printf("meslice2 = %v\n", meslice2)
  fmt.Printf("length = %d\n", len(meslice2))
  fmt.Printf("capacity = %d\n", cap(meslice2))
  }
```

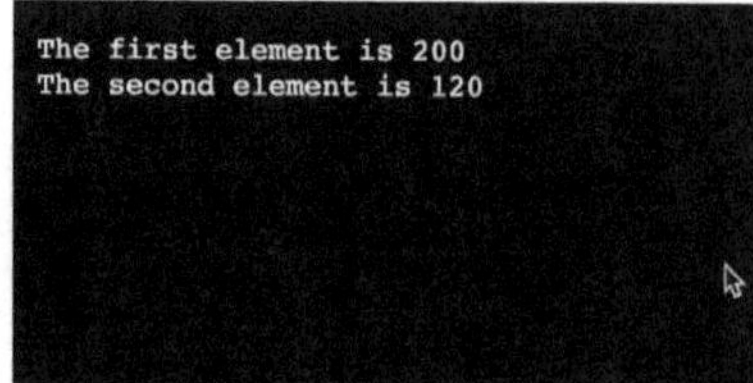

We can access a specific slice element by referring to the index number.
In Go, indexes start at 0. That means that [0] is the first element, [1] is the second element, etc.

```go
package main
import ("fmt")

func main() {
  marks := []int{200,120,390}

  fmt.Println("The first element is",marks[0])
  fmt.Println("The second element is",marks[1])
  }
```

We can also change a specific slice element by referring to the index number.

```go
package main
import ("fmt")

func main() {
  marks := []int{100,120,140}
  marks[1] = 100 // change of cell value
  fmt.Println("First cell",marks[0])
  fmt.Println("Third cell",marks[2])
  fmt.Println("Second cell edited value is ",marks[1])
}
```

```
First cell 100
Third cell 140
Second cell edited value is   100
```

We can append elements to the end of a slice using the append() function:

slice_name = append(slice_name, element1, element2, ...)

```go
package main
import ("fmt")

func main() {

// use of append to add to slice
  meslice1 := []int{11, 21, 31, 14, 15, 116}
  fmt.Printf("meslice1 = %v\n", meslice1)
  fmt.Printf("length = %d\n", len(meslice1))
  fmt.Printf("capacity = %d\n", cap(meslice1))

  meslice1 = append(meslice1, 200, 291)
  fmt.Printf("meslice1 = %v\n", meslice1)
  fmt.Printf("length = %d\n", len(meslice1))
  fmt.Printf("capacity = %d\n", cap(meslice1))
}
```

```
meslice1 = [11 21 31 14 15 116]
length = 6
capacity = 6
meslice1 = [11 21 31 14 15 116 200 291]
length = 8
capacity = 12
```

We can even append all the elements of one slice to another slice, using the append()
function:

Syntax

```
slice3 = append(slice1, slice2…)
package main
import ("fmt")

func main() {
// Defining three slices meslice1, meslice2, meslice3
  meslice1 := []int{12,22,32}
 meslice2 := []int{42,51,26}
 // Appending meslice3 via adding the two slices
  meslice3 := append(meslice1, meslice2...)
  fmt.Printf("\nElements of the appended slide are as follows \n")
  fmt.Printf("meslice3=%v\n", meslice3)
  fmt.Printf("length=%d\n", len(meslice3))
  fmt.Printf("capacity=%d\n", cap(meslice3))
}
```

```
Elements of the appended slide are as follows
meslice3=[12 22 32 42 51 26]
length=6
capacity=6
```

Memory Efficiency Using the copy() function:

The copy() function generates a new underlying array with only the required elements for the
slice. This accordingly reduces the memory used for the program.

Syntax

```
copy(dest, src)
```

Considering the above syntax: The copy() function takes in two slices *dest* and *src*, and copies data
from *src* to *dest*. It gives the number of elements copied.

```go
package main
import ("fmt")

func main() {
  marks := []int{110,111,112,113,114,115}
  // Original slice
  fmt.Printf("The original slice: marks = %v\n", marks)
  fmt.Printf("length = %d\n", len(marks))
  fmt.Printf("capacity = %d\n", cap(marks))

  // Create copy with only needed marks
  neededMarks := marks[:len(marks)-3]
  marksCopy := make([]int, len(neededMarks))
  copy(marksCopy, neededMarks)

  fmt.Printf("The copied Slice: marksCopy = %v\n", marksCopy)
  fmt.Printf("length = %d\n", len(marksCopy))
  fmt.Printf("capacity = %d\n", cap(marksCopy))
}
```

```
The original slice: marks = [110 111 112 113 114 115]
length = 6
capacity = 6
The copied Slice: marksCopy = [110 111 112]
length = 3
capacity = 3
```

Operators are used to performing operations on variables and values.

The + **operator** adds together two values, like in the example below:

```go
package main
import ("fmt")
func main() {

  var a = 115 + 215 // a is the sum of two numbers

  fmt.Println("The value of a is ", a)
}
```

```
The value of a is  330
```

Operator	Name	Description	Example
+	Addition	Adds together two values	x + y
-	Subtraction	Subtracts one value from another	x - y
*	Multiplication	Multiplies two values	x * y
/	Division	Divides one value by another	x / y
%	Modulus	Returns the division remainder	x % y
++	Increment	Increases the value of a variable by 1	x++
--	Decrement	Decreases the value of a variable by 1	x--

Operator	Example	Same As
=	x = 5	x = 5
+=	x += 3	x = x + 3
-=	x -= 3	x = x - 3
*=	x *= 3	x = x * 3
/=	x /= 3	x = x / 3
%=	x %= 3	x = x % 3
&=	x &= 3	x = x & 3
|=	x |= 3	x = x | 3
^=	x ^= 3	x = x ^ 3
>>=	x >>= 3	x = x >> 3
<<=	x <<= 3	x = x << 3

Operator	Name	Example
==	Equal to	x == y
!=	Not equal	x != y
>	Greater than	x > y
<	Less than	x < y
>=	Greater than or equal to	x >= y
<=	Less than or equal to	x <= y

Operator	Name	Description	Example
&&	Logical and	Returns true if both statements are true	x < 5 && x < 10
||	Logical or	Returns true if one of the statements is true	x < 5 || x < 4
!	Logical not	Reverse the result, returns false if the result is true	!(x < 5 && x < 10)

Operator	Name	Description	Example
&	AND	Sets each bit to 1 if both bits are 1	x & y
|	OR	Sets each bit to 1 if one of two bits is 1	x | y
^	XOR	Sets each bit to 1 if only one of two bits is 1	x ^ b
<<	Zero fill left shift	Shift left by pushing zeros in from the right	x << 2
>>	Signed right shift	Shift right by pushing copies of the leftmost bit in from the left, and let the rightmost bits fall off	x >> 2

GO Conditions

A condition can be either true or false.

Go supports the usual <u>comparison operators</u> from mathematics:

- Less than <
- Less than or equal <=
- Greater than >
- Greater than or equal >=
- Equal to ==
- Not equal to !=

Additionally, Go supports the usual <u>logical operators</u>:

- Logical AND &&
- Logical OR ||
- Logical NOT !

Conditional Statements of **GO**

Go has the following conditional statements:

- Use `if` to specify a block of code to be executed, if a specified condition is true
- Use `else` to specify a block of code to be executed if the same condition is false
- Use `else if` to specify a new condition to test, if the first condition is false
- Use `switch` to specify many alternative blocks of code to be executed

The if Statement

We make use of the `if` statement to specify a block of Go code to be executed if a condition is `true`.

Syntax

```
if condition {
    // code to be executed if condition is true
}
```

Example:

```
package main
import ("fmt")

func main() {
  if 200 < 218 {
    fmt.Println("200 is less than 218")
  }
}
```

```
200 is less than 218
```

The else Statement

Use the else statement to specify a block of code to be executed if the condition is false.

```go
package main

import ("fmt")

func main() {

age := 21
 if age < 18 {
  fmt.Println("You are not an adult")
 } else {
  fmt.Println("Hey Dear, You may vote now!")
 }
}
```

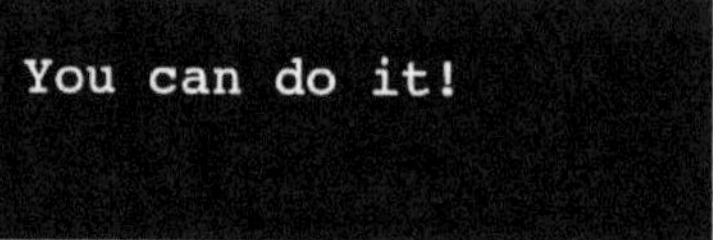

The else if Statement

The else if statement is used to specify a new condition if the first condition is false.

```go
package main
import ("fmt")

func main() {
 marks := 220
 if marks < 100 {
  fmt.Println("Sorry you have to re-appear!")
 } else if marks < 150 {
  fmt.Println("Sorry, Good day.")
 } else {
  fmt.Println("You can do it!")
 }
}
```

The Nested if Statement

We can very well have `if` statements inside `if` statements. This format is known as a nested if.

It has the following format:

```
if condition1 {
    // code to be executed if condition1 is true
  if condition2 {
      // code to be executed if both condition1 and condition2 are
true
  }
}
```

SAMPLE PROGRAM:

```
package main
import ("fmt")

func main() {
 number := 20 // Being defined number as 20
 if number >= 100 {
   fmt.Println("Hey Guys, Number is more than 100.")
   if number > 150 {
     fmt.Println("Hey Guys, Number is also more than 150.")
   }
 } else {
   fmt.Println("Hey Guys, Number is less than 100.")
 }
}
```

```
Hey Guys, Number is less than 100.
```

The switch Statement

We make use of the `switch` statement as a multiple branching statement. It only runs and executes the matched case and does not need a break statement of any kind.

It has the following syntax:

```
switch expression {
case x:
    // code block
case y:
    // code block
case z:
...
default:
    // code block
}
```

```go
package main
import ("fmt")
func main() {
// Program for entering a weekday number and returns the weekday!
  day := 2
  switch day {
  case 1:
    fmt.Println("It is Monday, Today!")
  case 2:
    fmt.Println("It is Tuesday, Today!")
  case 3:
    fmt.Println("It is Wednesday, Today!")
  case 4:
    fmt.Println("It is Thursday, Today!")
  case 5:
    fmt.Println("It is Friday, Today!")
  case 6:
    fmt.Println("It is Saturday, Today!")
  case 7:
    fmt.Println("Sunday")
  default:
        fmt.Println("Sorry wrong code entered")
  }
}
```


• The `default` keyword is optional. It specifies some code to run if there is no `case` match

The for loop is a branching statement of Go. It is used to execute a block of statements a specified number of times.

It has the following syntax:

```
for statement1; statement2; statement3 {
    // code to be executed for each iteration
}
```

statement1 is the initialized counter value.

statement2 evaluates the loop iteration. If it evaluates to FALSE, the loop ends.

statement3 Increases the counter.

```
package main
import ("fmt")

func main() {

// Loop to print even numbers from 1 to 15

fmt.Println("The even numbers from 1 to 15 are:")
  for i:=2; i <= 15; i+=2 {
    fmt.Println(i)
  }
}
```

```
The even numbers from 1 to 15 are:
2
4
6
8
10
12
14
```

The continue Statement

The `continue` statement is used to move the control to the next increment of the loop.

SAMPLE PROGRAM USING continue

```go
package main
import ("fmt")

func main() {
// Use of continue statement to exit the print if 5 is encountered
  for i:=1; i < 10; i++ {
    if i == 5 {
      continue
    }
    fmt.Println("The value of the loop variable is",i)
  }
}
```

```
The value of the loop variable is 1
The value of the loop variable is 2
The value of the loop variable is 3
The value of the loop variable is 4
The value of the loop variable is 6
The value of the loop variable is 7
The value of the loop variable is 8
The value of the loop variable is 9
```

The break Statement

The `break` statement is used to terminate the execution of the loop.

```go
package main
import ("fmt")

// use of break in for loop
func main() {
  for i:=0; i < 10; i++ {
    if i == 6 { // loop breaks if i encounters 6
      break
    }
    fmt.Println("The value of i, the loop variable is",i)
  }
}
```

```
The value of i, the loop variable is 0
The value of i, the loop variable is 1
The value of i, the loop variable is 2
The value of i, the loop variable is 3
The value of i, the loop variable is 4
The value of i, the loop variable is 5
```

Nested Loops

It is possible to place a loop inside another loop.

Here, the "inner loop" will be executed one time for each iteration of the "outer loop":

Sample Program

```go
package main
import ("fmt")
// use of nested loop
func main() {
 var public = [2]string{"learning", "reading"}
 var publication = [3]string{"language", "newspapers", "books"}
 for i:=0; i < len(publication); i++ {
  for j:=0; j < len(public); j++ {
   fmt.Println(publication[i],public[j])
  }
 }
}
```

```
language learning
language reading
newspapers learning
newspapers reading
books learning
books reading
```

Functions in Go

A function is a block of statements that can be used as many times in a program.

A function will not execute automatically when a page loads.

A function will be executed by a call to the function.

Steps To create or declare a function:

Use the `func` keyword.

- Specify a name for the function, followed by parentheses ().
- Include code within the curly braces {}.

The Functions are executed on call.

In the sample program given below, we create a function named "myWelcome()". The opening curly brace ({) indicates the beginning of the function code, and the closing curly brace (}) indicates the end of the function. The function displays the message "Hey Guys, welcome to the world of Go Programming!".

We call the function, using the function name: myWelcome() accordingly.

Sample Program

```
package main
import ("fmt")


// Create a function
func myWelcome() {
  fmt.Println("Hey Guys, welcome to the world of Go Programming!")
}


func main() {
  myWelcome() // call the function
}
```

```
Hey Guys, welcome to the world of Go Programming!
```

Arguments to a function:

Information can be passed to functions as a parameter. Parameters act as variables inside the function. Parameters and their types are specified after the function name, inside the parentheses as follows:

Sample Program

```
package main
import ("fmt")

func WName(getname string) {
  fmt.Println("Hello", getname, "Hope you are doing well")
}
func main() {
  WName("Abhishek") // calling the function using the parameter.
  WName("Shukla")
  WName("Abhinandan")
}
```

```
Hello Abhishek Hope you are doing well
Hello Shukla Hope you are doing well
Hello Abhinandan Hope you are doing well
```

Recursion Functions in Go

Go initiates recursion functions. A function is recursive if it calls itself and encounters an exit condition accordingly.

Sample Program:

```
package main
import ("fmt")
// using recursive function
func count(x int) int {
 if x == 0 {// dummy condition for end of recursion
  return 0
 }
 fmt.Println(x)
 return count(x - 1)
}

func main(){
 count(10)
}
```

```
10
9
8
7
6
5
4
3
2
1
```

Go Structures

A structure is used to create multiple members of different data types, into a single variable. A struct is a reserved word used for the same.

To declare a structure in Go, use the type and struct keywords as follows:

```
type RecordEmp struct {
  name string
  age int
  profile string
  salary int
}
```

In order to access any member of a structure, we make use of the dot operator (.) between the structure variable name and the structure member as follows:

```
EmpRecord.name = "Dheeraj"
```

Sample Program

```go
package main
import ("fmt")

type EmpRecord struct {
 name string
 age int
 profile string
 salary int
}

// end of structure declaration

func main() {
  var Record1 EmpRecord // defination of structure variable
  var Record2 EmpRecord

  // Record1 assignment
  Record1.name = "Abhishek"
  Record1.age = 40
  Record1.profile = "Teacher"
  Record1.salary = 65000

  // Record2 assignment
  Record2.name = "Shalini"
  Record2.age = 24
  Record2.profile = "Teacher"
  Record2.salary = 45000

  // Now Access and print Record1 information
  fmt.Println("Name: ", Record1.name)
  fmt.Println("Age: ", Record1.age)
  fmt.Println("Profile is : ", Record1.profile)
  fmt.Println("Salary: ", Record1.salary)

  // Now Access and print Record2 info
  fmt.Println("Name: ", Record2.name)
  fmt.Println("Age: ", Record2.age)
  fmt.Println("Profile is: ", Record2.profile)
  fmt.Println("Salary: ", Record2.salary)
}
```

Sample Output

```
Name:   Abhishek
Age:  40
Profile is :   Teacher
Salary:  65000
Name:  Shalini
Age:  24
Profile is:  Teacher
Salary:  45000
```

Go Maps

Maps are used to store data values in key:value pairs in Go Programming. Here, each element is a key: value pair and is an unordered and changeable collection that does not allow any duplicates. The length of the map is the number of its elements and can be obtained using the len() function.

To create an empty map, use the builtin make: `make(map[key-type]val-type)`.

Sample Program

```go
package main

import "fmt"

func main() {
        var employee = make(map[string]int)
        employee["Amrit"] = 100
        employee["Sumit"] = 200
        fmt.Println(employee)

        employeeList := make(map[string]int)
        employeeList["Sundaram"] = 104
        employeeList["Amrit"] = 205
        fmt.Println(employeeList)
}
```

```
map[Amrit:100 Sumit:200]
map[Amrit:205 Sundaram:104]
```

REVIEW

Go *Language, also known as GOLANG has pretty good features which make it a widely-used programming language. It grows faster than any other language in view, it can be compiled into many platforms, has multiple cores, has concurrency and routines and above all is very easy to maintain.*

Some of its wide references include

https://play.golang.org/

https://tour.golang.org

https://gobyexample.com/ among others.

Some of the widely acclaimed applications of GOLANG reflect via Twitter, Youtube and Dropbox.

Twitter's new system architecture for mobile has a service application written in Go that actually helps to handle five billion requests per day. In addition, Youtube uses GOLANG to manage the MYSQL server. Dropbox, on the other hand, has changed the stacks from python to Go in particular.

The language installation goes as follows:

Download from http://golang.org/doc/install

Unzip from the folder

Set the Environment variables:

GOROOT=> Installation directory of Go (Windows=c:\windows\)

PATH=>$GOROOT; (library folders.....);

It nourishes as a multi-platform language, static in nature, Type-safe/ Memory-safe, provides garbage collection and is fast in the compilation. A very important feature is its derivation from Gopher, created by Google Engineers. It is a language for the multi-core processor and searches faster with ease of programming and compilation.

About The Author

Dheeraj Mehrotra, MS, MPhil, Ph.D. (Education Management) honoris causa., a white and a yellow belt in SIX SIGMA, a Certified NLP Business Diploma holder, is an Educational Innovator, Author, with expertise in Six Sigma In Education, Academic Audits, Neuro-Linguistic Programming (NLP), Total Quality Management In Education, an Experiential Educator, a CBSE Resource towards School Assessment (SQAA), CCE, JIT, Five S, and KAIZEN. He has authored over 40 books on Computer Science for ICSE/ ISC/ CBSE Students, over 60 books of academic interest for the field of education excellence, and Six Sigma. A former Principal at De Indian Public School, New Delhi, (INDIA) with an ample teaching experience of over Two Decades, he is a certified Trainer for Quality Circles/ TQM in Education and QCI Standards for School Accreditation/ Six Sigma in Education. He has also been honoured with the President of India's National Teacher Award in the year 2006 and the Best Science Teacher State Award (By the Ministry of Science and Technology, State of UP), Innovation in Education for his inception of Six Sigma In Education by Education Watch, New Delhi and Education World- Best Teacher Award, BOLT Learner Teacher Award by Air India, 'Innovation in Education Award 2016' by Higher Education Forum (HEF), Gujarat Chapter, among others. He has developed over 150 FREE EDUCATIONAL MOBILE Apps for the Google Play Store exclusively for Teachers, Students, and Parents. This work has been recognized by the LIMCA BOOK OF RECORDS & INDIA BOOK OF RECORDS as the only Indian to draw that feast. Dr Mehrotra is presently working as a PRINCIPAL at KUNWARS GLOBAL SCHOOL, Lucknow, in India. He has conducted over 1000 workshops globally on "Excellence In Education" integrated with Total Quality Management and Six Sigma, Technology Integration in Education (TIE), Developing towards being ROCKSTAR TEACHERS, including Cyberspace, Cyber Security, Classroom Management, School Leadership &

Management, and Innovative teaching within classrooms via Mind Maps, NLP and Experiential Learning in Academics. He is an active TEDx speaker and can be viewed on the youtube TEDx channel. As a premium UDEMY Instructor, he has also developed over 450 courses and is catering to over 8 Lakh students from 180 plus countries.

www.authordheerajmehrotra.com

It is worth knowing now!
digital
body
Language
Dr Dheeraj Mehrotra

#Amazon!

BASICS OF
ARTIFICIAL
INTELLIGENCE
&
MACHINE
LEARNING
Dr. DHEERAJ MEHROTRA
BY
NATIONAL
AWARDEE
EDUCATOR
NOW AVAILABLE AT
amazon
authordheerajmehrotra.com

www.ingramcontent.com/pod-product-compliance
Lightning Source LLC
Chambersburg PA
CBHW061337120726
48001CB00002B/915